PENGUIN BOOKS

DOG SONGS

Born in a small town in Ohio, Mary Oliver published her first book of poetry in 1963 at the age of 28. Over the course of her long career, she received numerous awards. Her fourth book, *American Primitive*, won the Pulitzer Prize for Poetry in 1984. She led workshops and held residencies at various colleges and universities, including Bennington College, where she held the Catharine Osgood Foster Chair for Distinguished Teaching. She died in 2019.

Dog Songs

Thirty-five

Dog Songs

and

One Essay

MARY OLIVER

PENGUIN BOOKS

PENGUIN BOOKS
An imprint of Penguin Random House LLC
penguinrandomhouse.com

First published in the United States of America by Penguin Press,
an imprint of Penguin Random House LLC, 2013
Published in Penguin Books 2015

THE LIBRARY OF CONGRESS HAS CATALOGED THE
HARDCOVER EDITION AS FOLLOWS:
Oliver, Mary.
Dog Songs : Thirty-five Dog Songs and One Essay / Mary Oliver.
pages cm
ISBN 978-1-59420-478-4 (hc.)
ISBN 978-0-14-312583-9 (pbk.)
1. Dogs—Poetry. 2. Human-animal relationships—Poetry. I. Title.
PS3565.L5D64 2013
811'.54—dc23
2013028114

Printed in the United States of America
20 22 24 26 28   27 25 23 21

Illustrations by John Burgoyne
Book design by Claire Naylon Vaccaro

For Anne Taylor and Martin Michaelson

CONTENTS

Dog Songs

HOW IT BEGINS

A puppy is a puppy is a puppy.
He's probably in a basket with a bunch
   of other puppies.
Then he's a little older and he's nothing
   but a bundle of longing.
He doesn't even understand it.

Then someone picks him up and says,
   "I want this one."

HOW IT IS WITH US, AND
HOW IT IS WITH THEM

We become religious,

then we turn from it,

then we are in need and maybe we turn back.

We turn to making money,

then we turn to the moral life,

then we think about money again.

We meet wonderful people, but lose them
in our busyness.

We're, as the saying goes, all over the place.

Steadfastness, it seems,

is more about dogs than about us.

One of the reasons we love them so much.

IF YOU ARE HOLDING
THIS BOOK

You may not agree, you may not care, but
if you are holding this book you should know
that of all the sights I love in this world—
and there are plenty—very near the top of
the list is this one: dogs without leashes.

EVERY DOG'S STORY

I have a bed, my very own.
It's just my size.
And sometimes I like to sleep alone
with dreams inside my eyes.

But sometimes dreams are dark and wild and creepy
and I wake and am afraid, though I don't know why.
But I'm no longer sleepy
and too slowly the hours go by.

So I climb on the bed where the light of the moon
is shining on your face
and I know it will be morning soon.

Everybody needs a safe place.

THE STORM (BEAR)

Now through the white orchard my little dog
  romps, breaking the new snow
  with wild feet.
Running here running there, excited,
  hardly able to stop, he leaps, he spins
until the white snow is written upon
  in large, exuberant letters,
a long sentence, expressing
  the pleasures of the body in this world.

Oh, I could not have said it better
  myself.

CONVERSATIONS

1.

Said Bear, "I know I'm supposed to keep my eye
on you, but it's difficult the way you
lag behind and keep talking to people."

Well, how can you be keeping your eye on me
when you're half a mile ahead?

"True," said Bear. "But I'm thinking of you
all the time."

2.

I had to go away for a few days so I called
the kennel and made an appointment. I guess
Bear overheard the conversation.

. . .

"Love and company," said Bear, "are the adornments
that change everything. I know they'll be
nice to me, but I'll be sad, sad, sad."
And pitifully he wrung his paws.

I cancelled the trip.

LUKE'S JUNKYARD SONG

I was born in a junkyard,
not even on a bundle of rags
or the seat of an old wrecked car
but the dust below.

But when my eyes opened
I could crawl to the edge and see
the moving grass and the trees
and this I began to dream on,
though the worms were eating me.

And at night through the twists of metal
I could see a single star—one, not even two.
Its light was a thing of wonder,
and I learned something precious
that would also be good for you.

. . .

Though the worms kept biting and pinching
I fell in love with this star.
I stared at it every night—
that light so clear and far.

Listen, a junkyard puppy
learns quickly how to dream.
Listen, whatever you see and love—
that's where you are.

LUKE

I had a dog
    who loved flowers.
        Briskly she went
            through the fields,

yet paused
    for the honeysuckle
        or the rose,
            her dark head

and her wet nose
    touching
        the face
            of every one

with its petals
    of silk,
        with its fragrance
            rising

. . .

into the air
   where the bees,
      their bodies
         heavy with pollen,

hovered—
   and easily
      she adored
         every blossom,

not in the serious,
   careful way
      that we choose
         this blossom or that blossom—

the way we praise or don't praise—
   the way we love
      or don't love—
         but the way

we long to be—
   that happy
      in the heaven of earth—
         that wild, that loving.

HER GRAVE

She would come back, dripping thick water, from the
green bog.
She would fall at my feet, she would draw the black skin
from her gums, in a hideous and wonderful smile—
and I would rub my hands over her pricked ears and her
cunning elbows,
and I would hug the barrel of her body, amazed at the
unassuming perfect arch of her neck.

It took four of us to carry her into the woods.
We did not think of music,
but anyway, it began to rain
slowly.

Her wolfish, invitational half-pounce.

Her great and lordly satisfaction at having chased
something.

. . .

My great and lordly satisfaction at her splash
of happiness as she barged
through the pitch pines swiping my face with her
wild, slightly mossy tongue.

Does the hummingbird think he himself invented his
    crimson throat?
He is wiser than that, I think.

A dog lives fifteen years, if you're lucky.

Do the cranes crying out in the high clouds
think it is all their own music?

A dog comes to you and lives with you in your own house,
    but you
do not therefore own her, as you do not own the rain, or the
trees, or the laws which pertain to them.

. . .

Does the bear wandering in the autumn up the side of
    the hill
think all by herself she has imagined the refuge and the
    refreshment
of her long slumber?

A dog can never tell you what she knows from the
smells of the world, but you know, watching her,
    that you know
almost nothing.

Does the water snake with his backbone of diamonds think
the black tunnel on the bank of the pond is a palace
of his own making?

She roved ahead of me through the fields, yet would come
    back,
or wait for me, or be somewhere.

Now she is buried under the pines.

Nor will I argue it, or pray for anything but modesty, and
not to be angry.

. . .

Through the trees there is the sound of the wind,
    palavering.

The smell of the pine needles, what is it but a taste
of the infallible energies?

How strong was her dark body!
How apt is her grave place.

How beautiful is her unshakable sleep.

Finally,
the slick mountains of love break
over us.

BENJAMIN, WHO CAME FROM WHO KNOWS WHERE

What shall I do?
When I pick up the broom
   he leaves the room.
When I fuss with kindling he
   runs for the yard.
Then he's back, and we
   hug for a long time.
In his low-to-the-ground chest
   I can hear his heart slowing down.
Then I rub his shoulders and
   kiss his feet
and fondle his long hound ears.
   Benny, I say,
don't worry. I also know the way
   the old life haunts the new.

THE DOG HAS RUN OFF
AGAIN (BENJAMIN)

and I should start shouting his name
and clapping my hands,
but it has been raining all night
and the narrow creek has risen
is a tawny turbulence is rushing along
over the mossy stones
is surging forward
with a sweet loopy music
and therefore I don't want to entangle it
with my own voice
calling summoning
my little dog to hurry back
look, the sunlight and the shadows are chasing each other
listen how the wind swirls and leaps and dives up and down
who am I to summon his hard and happy body
his four white feet that love to wheel and pedal
through the dark leaves
to come back to walk by my side, obedient.

HOLDING ON TO BENJAMIN

No use to tell him
that he

and the raccoon are brothers.
You have your soft ideas about nature

he has others,
and they are full of his

white teeth
and lip that curls, sometimes,

horribly.
You love

this earnest dog,
but also you admire the raccoon

and Lord help you in your place
of hope and improbables.

. . .

To the black-masked gray one:
Run! you say,

and just as urgently, to the dog:
Stay!

and he won't or he will,
depending

on more things than I could name.
He's sure he's right

and you, so tangled in your mind,
are wrong,

though patient and pacific.
And you are downcast.

And it's his eyes, not yours,
that are clear and bright.

THE POETRY TEACHER

The university gave me a new, elegant
classroom to teach in. Only one thing,
they said. You can't bring your dog.
It's in my contract, I said. (I had
made sure of that.)

We bargained and I moved to an old
classroom in an old building. Propped
the door open. Kept a bowl of water
in the room. I could hear Ben among
other voices barking, howling in the
distance. Then they would all arrive—
Ben, his pals, maybe an unknown dog
or two, all of them thirsty and happy.
They drank, they flung themselves down
among the students. The students loved
it. They all wrote thirsty, happy poems.

BAZOUGEY

Where goes he now, that dark little dog
    who used to come down the road barking and shining?
He's gone now, from the world of particulars,
    the singular, the visible.

So, that deepest sting: sorrow. Still,
    is he gone from us entirely, or is he
a part of that other world, everywhere?

Come with me into the woods where spring is
    advancing, as it does, no matter what,
not being singular or particular, but one
    of the forever gifts, and certainly visible.

See how the violets are opening, and the leaves
    unfolding, the streams gleaming and the birds
    singing. What does it make you think of?
His shining curls, his honest eyes, his
    beautiful barking.

ROPES

IN THE OLD DAYS dogs in our town roamed freely. But the old ways changed.

One morning a puppy arrived in our yard with a length of rope hanging from his collar. He played with our dogs; eventually he vanished. But the next morning he showed up again, with a different rope attached. This happened for a number of days—he appeared, he was playful and friendly, and always accompanied by a chewed-through rope.

Just at that time we were moving to another house, which we finished doing all in one evening. A day or so later, on a hunch, I drove back to the old house and found him lying in the grass by our door. I put him in the car and showed him where our new house was. "Do your best," I said.

He stayed around for a while, then was gone. But there he was the next morning at the new house. Rope dangling. Later that day his owner appeared—with his papers from the Bideawee home, and a leash. "His name is Sammy," she said. "And he's yours."

As Sammy grew older he began to roam around the town and,

as a result, began to be caught by the dog officer. Eventually, of course, we were summoned to court, which, we learned quickly, was not a place in which to argue. We were told to build a fence. Which we did.

But it turned out that Sammy could not only chew through ropes, he could also climb fences. So his roaming continued.

But except for the dog officer, Sammy never got into trouble; he made friends. He wouldn't fight with other dogs, he just seemed to stay awhile in someone's yard and, if possible, to say hello to the owners. People began to call us to come and get him before the dog officer saw him. Some took him into their houses to hide him from the law. Once a woman on the other end of town called; when I got there she said, "Can you wait just a few minutes? I'm making him some scrambled eggs."

I could tell many more stories about Sammy, they're endless. But I'll just tell you the unexpected, joyful conclusion. The dog officer resigned! And the next officer was a different sort; he too remembered and missed the old days. So when he found Sammy he would simply call him into his truck and drive him home. In this way, he lived a long and happy life, with many friends.

This is Sammy's story. But I also think there are one or two poems in it somewhere. Maybe it's what life was like in this dear town years ago, and how a lot of us miss it.

Or maybe it's about the wonderful things that may happen if you break the ropes that are holding you.

PERCY

Our new dog, named for the beloved poet,
ate a book which unfortunately we had
    left unguarded.
Fortunately it was the *Bhagavad Gita*,
of which many copies are available.
Every day now, as Percy grows
into the beauty of his life, we touch
his wild, curly head and say,

"Oh, wisest of little dogs."

SCHOOL

You're like a little wild thing

that was never sent to school.

Sit, I say, and you jump up.

Come, I say, and you go galloping down the sand

to the nearest dead fish

with which you perfume your sweet neck.

It is summer.

How many summers does a little dog have?

Run, run, Percy.

This is our school.

LITTLE DOG'S RHAPSODY IN
THE NIGHT

He puts his cheek against mine
and makes small, expressive sounds.
And when I'm awake, or awake enough

he turns upside down, his four paws
   in the air
and his eyes dark and fervent.

"Tell me you love me," he says.

"Tell me again."

Could there be a sweeter arrangement? Over and over
he gets to ask.
I get to tell.

TIME PASSES

And now Percy is getting brazen.
"Let's down the beach, baby," he says.
"Let's shake it with a little barking.
Let's find dead things, and explore them,
by mouth, if possible."

Or maybe the leavings of Paul's horse (after which,
forgive me for mentioning it, he is fond of kissing).

Ah, this is the thing that comes to each of us.
The child grows up.
And, according to our own ideas, is practically asunder.

I understand it.
I struggle to celebrate.
I say, with a stiff upper lip familiar to many:

Just look at that curly-haired child now, he's his own man.

UNTITLED

Just before Percy had his operation
he had one long rendezvous with a
little dog named Penny. As it happened
there was no result. But, oh, how
Percy smiled and smiled all the way
home.

PERCY WAKES ME

Percy wakes me and I am not ready.

He has slept all night under the covers.

Now he's eager for action: a walk, then breakfast.

So I hasten up. He is sitting on the kitchen counter
   where he is not supposed to be.

How wonderful you are, I say. How clever, if you
  needed me,

     to wake me.

He thought he would hear a lecture and deeply
   his eyes begin to shine.

He tumbles onto the couch for more compliments.

He squirms and squeals; he has done something
  that he needed

     and now he hears that it is okay.

I scratch his ears, I turn him over
   and touch him everywhere. He is

wild with the okayness of it. Then we walk, then
  he has breakfast, and he is happy.

. . .

This is a poem about Percy.

This is a poem about more than Percy.

Think about it.

THE SWEETNESS OF DOGS

What do you say, Percy? I am thinking
of sitting out on the sand to watch
the moon rise. It's full tonight.
So we go

and the moon rises, so beautiful it
makes me shudder, makes me think about
time and space, makes me take
measure of myself: one iota
pondering heaven. Thus we sit, myself

thinking how grateful I am for the moon's
perfect beauty and also, oh! how rich
it is to love the world. Percy, meanwhile,
leans against me and gazes up into
my face. As though I were just as wonderful
as the perfect moon.

PERCY SPEAKS WHILE I AM
DOING TAXES

First of all, I do not want to be doing this.
Second of all, Percy does not want me
    to be doing this,
bent over the desk like a besieged person
    with a dull pencil and innumerable lists
        of numbers.

Outside the water is blue, the sky is clear,
    the tide rising.
Percy, I say, this has to be done. This is
    essential. I'll be finished eventually.

"Keep me in your thoughts," he replies. "Just because
    I can't count to ten doesn't mean
I don't remember yesterday, or anticipate today.
I'll give you ten more minutes," and he does.
    Then shouts—who could resist—his
        favorite words: Let's go!

PERCY, WAITING FOR RICKY

Your friend is coming, I say
to Percy and name a name

and he runs to the door, his
wide mouth in its laugh-shape,

and waves, since he has one, his tail.
Emerson, I am trying to live,

as you said we must, the examined life.
But there are days I wish

there was less in my head to examine,
not to speak of the busy heart. How

would it be to be Percy, I wonder, not
thinking, not weighing anything, just running forward.

PERCY (2002–2009)

This—I said to Percy when I had left
    our bed and gone
out onto the living room couch where
he found me apparently doing nothing—this
    is called *thinking*.
It's something people do,
not being entirely children of the earth,
    like a dog or a tree or a flower.

His eyes questioned such an activity.
"Well, okay," he said. "If you say so. Whatever
it is. Actually
    I like kissing better."

And next to me,
tucked down his curly head
and, sweet as a flower, slept.

"FOR I WILL CONSIDER MY
DOG PERCY"

For I will consider my dog Percy.

For he was made small but brave of heart.

For if he met another dog he would kiss her in kindness.

For when he slept he snored only a little.

For he could be silly and noble in the same moment.

For when he spoke he remembered the trumpet and when
he scratched he struck the floor like a drum.

For he ate only the finest food and drank only the
purest of water, yet would nibble of dead fish also.

For he came to me impaired and therefore certain of
short life, yet thoroughly rejoiced in each day.

For he took his medicines without argument.

.   .   .

For he played easily with the neighborhood's bull
   mastiff.

For when he came upon mud he splashed through it.

*For he was an instrument for the children to learn
   benevolence upon.*

For he listened to poems as well as love-talk.

For when he sniffed it was as if he were being
   pleased by every part of the world.

For when he sickened he rallied as many times as
   he could.

For he was a mixture of gravity and waggery.

For we humans can seek self-destruction in ways
   he never dreamed of.

For he took actions both cunning and reckless, yet
   refused always to offer himself to be admonished.

. . .

For his sadness though without words was
 understandable.

*For there was nothing sweeter than his peace
 when at rest.*

*For there was nothing brisker than his life when
 in motion.*

For he was of the tribe of Wolf.

For when I went away he would watch for me at
 the window.

For he loved me.

For he suffered before I found him, and never
 forgot it.

For he loved Anne.

For when he lay down to enter sleep he did not argue
 about whether or not God made him.

. . .

For he could fling himself upside down and laugh
   a true laugh.

For he loved his friend Ricky.

For he would dig holes in the sand and then let
   Ricky lie in them.

For often I see his shape in the clouds and this is
   a continual blessing.

THE FIRST TIME PERCY CAME BACK

The first time Percy came back
he was not sailing on a cloud.
He was loping along the sand as though
he had come a great way.
"Percy," I cried out, and reached to him—
       those white curls—
but he was unreachable. As music
is present yet you can't touch it.
"Yes, it's all different," he said.
"You're going to be very surprised."
But I wasn't thinking of that. I only
wanted to hold him. "Listen," he said.
"I miss that too.
And now you'll be telling stories
       of my coming back
and they won't be false, and they won't be true,
but they'll be real."
And. then, as he used to, he said, "Let's go!"
And we walked down the beach together.

RICKY TALKS ABOUT
TALKING

Ricky, can you explain how it is that
Anne and I can talk with you, as we did
with Percy too, and we all understand
each other? Is it a kind of miracle?

"It's no miracle," said Ricky. "It's
actually simple. When you or Anne talk,
I listen. When I talk you listen, as
you did with Percy."

Of course we listen!

"No, I mean *really* listen. Here's a
story, and you don't have to visit many
houses to find it. One person is talking,
the other one is not really listening.
Someone can look like they are but they're
actually thinking about something they
want to say, or their minds are just

wandering. Or they're looking at that little box people hold in their hands these days. And people get discouraged, so they quit trying. And the very quiet people, you may have noticed, are often the sad people."

Ricky, you have really thought about this. So we can talk together because we really listen, and that's because . . .

"Yes, because we care."

THE WICKED SMILE

"Please, please, I think I haven't eaten
for days."

What? Ricky, you had a huge supper.

"I did? My stomach doesn't remember.
Oh, I think I'm fading away. Please
make me breakfast and I'll tell you
something you don't know."

He ate rapidly.

Okay, I said. What were you going to
tell me?

He smiled the wicked smile. "Before we
came over, Anne already gave me my breakfast,"
he said.

. . .

Be prepared. A dog is adorable and noble.
A dog is a true and loving friend. A dog
is also a hedonist.

THE TRAVELER

Ricky, your ancesters are from Cuba,
   right?

Says Ricky, "So I'm told."

But you were born in Florida?

"I was a baby, how would I know?
   But that's what I'm told."

And you've lived in Massachusetts and
   other states and also Mexico and
   now Florida again, and heaven knows
   what other places you may travel to.
   Are you an American, or what?

He shrugged his shoulders casually and
   smiled. *"Je suis un chien du monde,"*
   he said.

SHOW TIME

And here come the dogs. Brushed, trimmed,
polished.

"What on earth have they done to them!"
said Ricky. "They're half shaved. And
wearing pillows on their heads. And
where are their tails?"

It's the rules, I said.

"And look at those women trying to run.
They sure don't look like you."

Thank you, I said.

"I'm getting a headache looking at this.
I have to bark!" And he began.

It does no good to bark at the television,
I said. I've tried it too. So he stopped.

. . .

"If I ever meet one of these dogs I'm going to invite him to come here, where he can be a proper dog."

Okay, I said. But remember, you can't fix everything in the world for everybody.

"However," said Ricky, "you can't do anything at all unless you begin. Haven't I heard you say that once or twice, or maybe a hundred times?"

A BAD DAY

Ricky, why are you barking and trying
to rip up the couch? Can't you settle
down? It's been a long day.

"It sure has. First you forgot to take
me out. Then you went to the market
and heaven knows where else. And my
dinner was late. And our walk was
short. And now you're supposed to
be on the floor playing with me but,
no, you're doing something else. So I
thought I'd give this couch a little
distress."

Well, don't. Be a good boy.

"Honestly, what do you expect? Like
you I'm not perfect, I'm only human."

HENRY

"What is that?" said Ricky as Henry
came through the door.

That's Henry, I said. He's a bulldog
and he's come to stay with us with my
friend Linda.

"He's a horse," said Ricky. "Already my
heart is pounding."

Yes, he's big, he's supposed to be.
Say hello to him.

"Really. Well hello, Henry. I hope
you don't gobble up all my toys."

Henry: Snort, snort.

Ricky: (to me) "He's not very good with
words, is he."

. . .

Henry, after another snort, clambered
onto the couch.

Ricky shouted, "There isn't
room for both of us!"

Sure there is. Just move over, and
give yourself a little time to know
him.

Ricky sat closer, but with a nervous
look.

It was a wonderful week. My friend
and I talked, we walked on the beach,
Ricky and Henry went swimming, they
dug a hole together, no toys got
eaten.

Finally they had to leave. Ricky by
that time was friendly with limping,
lumbering, fifteen-year-old Henry.

. . .

"Bye, bye, Henry," he said.

"Snort, snort," said Henry.

Then they were gone.

Said Ricky, "He really is as big as
a horse, but actually a very sweet
horse. I hope he comes again."

HOW A LOT OF US BECOME FRIENDS

One day on the beach Ricky met a dog
just his size. Her name is Lucy,
and she is very pretty.
"Wow," said Ricky.

Naturally, I met Lucy's mother, Theresa,
at the same time.

It happens that Ricky's full name is
Ricky Ricardo, so how could Ricky and
Lucy not take to each other? In fact,
they became quite tight. It wasn't
a good day if they didn't see each
other.

So how could Theresa and I not start
on that day to become friends?

YOU NEVER KNOW WHERE
A CONVERSATION IS
GOING TO GO

Said Ricky to me one day, "Why is it you
don't have a tail?"

Well, I just don't. Maybe once upon a time
I had one, but not anymore.

"What happened? Did you have an accident?"

No, no. Things change. Sometimes. Over
time.

"You mean, maybe sometime I won't get a walk,
I won't get dinner? I won't get hugs? That's
scary, plain scary."

No, no, it takes a really long time. In
fact, some things change, over time, and
some don't.

. . .

"Well, how do I know what's what?"

Day by day, Ricky. You find out.
Has anything changed that troubles you?

"Actually, nothing. I like everything a lot,
every day."

Well, see? Just keep on liking things.
And praying.

"I don't know anything about that."

Yes you do. Every time you wake up and
love your life and the world, you're
praying, my dear boy. I'm sure of it.

DOG TALK

HE IS AHEAD OF ME in the fields, poking about in the grass. By the time I reach him the last of the newborn field mice are disappearing down his throat. His eyes roll upward to read my mood—praise, amusement or disapproval—but I only touch his head casually and walk on. Let him make his own judgment. The mice construct thick, cupped nests deep in the grass from which they travel along a multitude of tunneled paths—to the creek perhaps, or into the orchard to find a bruised apple or a leaf of mint, or buckberries. Then they hurry home again, to the peep and swirl of their nestlings. But these babes have been crunched on Ben's molars, have begun the descent through darkness and acids toward transformation. I hope they were well crunched.

At home Ben "wolfs" his food, as the saying goes. He barely lifts his face from the bowl, scarcely breathes until all is gone. He came to us a lost dog, down from the Blue Ridge, and certainly he had known trouble and probably, at least for a while, hunger. He came with a split tongue, a wound mysterious and long healed, made perhaps on a roughly opened can, or by another dog during trough feeding. It is one of the secrets we will never know. The

rip is an inch long, at the front of the tongue, not quite centered. Now the tongue brims forward on its final slide in two directions, or hangs to both sides of his right fang tooth, which stands above the mossy bulk of the tongue like a white bird on a pink sea.

Other quirks and mannerisms, frights and anxieties, Ben brought with him, and has kept. Mostly he wants reasonable things—quiet, security, both M. and me within sight. He is frightened of lightning, brooms, kindling, backfire, and trucks generally. He loves fields, freedom, rabbit-smell, rides in the car, lots of food. I think he can drink a gallon of water at a single stint. I think he can run for eight hours without halt. Or, he used to.

Where's Ben?
Down in the creek, getting muddy.

Where's Ben?
Out in the field eating mice again.

Where's Ben?
Upstairs in his bedroom sleeping on his four
pillows and his blue blanket.

Of night and the dog: you cannot elaborate the dark thickness of it as he can, you cannot separate the rich, rank threads as they

make their way through the grasses: mouse, vole, mink, nails of the fox then the thin stream of his urine, drops sticking to the grass blades, necklace of pale gold. And the rabbit—his paw smell, his juice or a single strand of fur, or a bleat from a gland under the white tail, or a bead of excrement, black pearls dropped off here and there. I have seen Ben place his nose meticulously into the shallow dampness of a deer's hoofprint and shut his eyes as if listening. But it is smell he is listening to. The wild, high music of smell, that we know so little about.

*

Tonight Ben charges up the yard; Bear follows. They run into the field and are gone. A soft wind, like a belt of silk, wraps the house. I follow them to the end of the field where I hear the long-eared owl, at wood's edge, in one of the tall pines. All night the owl will sit there inventing his catty racket, except when he opens pale wings and drifts moth-like over the grass. I have seen both dogs look up as the bird floats by, and I suppose the field mouse hears it too, in the pebble of his tiny heart. Though I hear nothing.

*

Bear is small and white with a curly tail. He was meant to be idle and pretty but learned instead to love the world, and to romp roughly with the big dogs. The brotherliness of the two, Ben and Bear, increases with each year. They have their separate habits,

their own favorite sleeping places, for example, yet each worries without letup if the other is missing. They both bark rapturously and in support of each other. They both sneeze to express pleasure, and yawn in humorous admittance of embarrassment. In the car, when we are getting close to home and the smell of the ocean begins to surround them, they both sit bolt upright and hum.

> With what vigor
> and intention to please himself
> the little white dog
> flings himself into every puddle
> on the muddy road.

Some things are unchangeably wild, others are stolidly tame. The tiger is wild, and the coyote, and the owl. I am tame, you are tame. There are wild things that have been altered, but only into a semblance of tameness, it is no real change. But the dog lives in both worlds. Ben is devoted, he hates the door between us, is afraid of separation. But he had, for a number of years, a dog friend to whom he was also loyal. Every day they and a few others gathered into a noisy gang, and some of their games were bloody. Dog is docile, and then forgets. Dog promises then forgets. Voices call him. Wolf faces appear in dreams. He finds himself running over incredible lush or barren stretches of land, nothing any of us

has ever seen. Deep in the dream, his paws twitch, his lip lifts. The dreaming dog leaps through the underbrush, enters the earth through a narrow tunnel, and is home. The dog wakes and the disturbance in his eyes when you say his name is a recognizable cloud. How glad he is to see you, and he sneezes a little to tell you so.

But ah! the falling-back, fading dream where he was almost *there* again, in the pure, rocky, weather-ruled beginning. Where he was almost wild again and knew nothing else but that life, no other possibility. A world of trees and dogs and the white moon, the nest, the breast, the heart-warming milk! The thick-mantled ferocity at the end of the tunnel, known as father, a warrior he himself would grow to be.

Dog promises and then forgets, blame him not. The tooth glitters in the ridged mouth. The fur lifts along the spine. He lifts a leg and sprays a radiant mist over a stone, or a dead toad, or somebody's hat. He understands what is wanted; and tries, and tries again, and is good for a long time, and then forgets.

*

And it is exceedingly short, his galloping life. Dogs die so soon. I have my stories of that grief, no doubt many of you do also. It is almost a failure of will, a failure of love, to let them grow old—or so it feels. We would do anything to keep them with us, and to keep them young. The one gift we cannot give.

Baba, Chico, Obediah, Phoebe, Abigail, Emily, Emma, Josie, Pushpa, Chester, Zara, Lucky, Benjamin, Bear, Henry, Atisha, Ollie, Beulah, Gussie, Cody, Angelina, Lightning, Holly, Suki, Buster, Bazougey, Tyler, Milo, Magic, Taffy, Buffy, Thumper, Katie, Petey, Bennie, Edie, Max, Luke, Jessie, Keesha, Jasper, Brick, Briar Rose.

Bear lifts his head and listens brightly. He growls in excitement and runs to the window to look. Is it a trick or a gift, my saying aloud the names of the dogs without producing the dogs? All winter he will hurry to listen to this puzzle, this strange and wonderful pleasure.

But I want to extol not the sweetness nor the placidity of the dog, but the wilderness out of which he cannot step entirely, and from which we benefit. For wilderness is our first home too, and in our wild ride into modernity with all its concerns and problems we need also all the good attachments to that origin that we can keep or restore. Dog is one of the messengers of that rich and still magical first world. The dog would remind us of the pleasures of the body with its graceful physicality, and the acuity and rapture

of the senses, and the beauty of forest and ocean and rain and our own breath. There is not a dog that romps and runs but we learn from him.

The other dog—the one that all its life walks leashed and obedient down the sidewalk—is what a chair is to a tree. It is a possession only, the ornament of a human life. Such dogs can remind us of nothing large or noble or mysterious or lost. They cannot make us sweeter or more kind.

Only unleashed dogs can do that. They are a kind of poetry themselves when they are devoted not only to us but to the wet night, to the moon and the rabbit-smell in the grass and their own bodies leaping forward.

Thunder that is still too far away for us to hear presses down on Ben's ears and he wakes us and leans hot and chesty first against M., then against me, and listens to our slow, warm words that mean we love him. But when the storm has passed, he is brave again and wants to go out. We open the door and he glides away without a backward glance. It is early, in the blue and grainy air we can just see him running along the edge of the water, into the first pink suggestion of sunrise. And we are caught by the old affinity, a joyfulness—his great and seemly pleasure in the physical world. Because of the dog's joyfulness, our own is increased. It is

no small gift. It is not the least reason why we should honor as well as love the dog of our own life, and the dog down the street, and all the dogs not yet born. What would the world be like without music or rivers or the green and tender grass? What would this world be like without dogs?

NOTE

The poem "For I Will Consider My Dog Percy" is obviously derivative of Christopher Smart's poem "For I Will Consider My Cat Jeoffry." It is in no way an imitation except in style. Jeoffry wins entirely. But for a few days I simply stood upon the shoulders of that wondrous poem and began to think about Percy.

The lines in italics, except for the exchange of names and altering of verb tense from present to past, are Christopher Smart's own, and in that way are acknowledged to be so.

M. O.

CREDITS

"Benjamin, Who Came from Who Knows Where" was first published in *The Bark* magazine, July/August 2008. "Bazougey" was first published in *The Bark* magazine, January/February 2007.

Grateful acknowledgment is made for permission to reprint the following works:

"The Storm" from *Winter Hours: Prose, Prose Poems and Poems* by Mary Oliver. Copyright © 1999 by Mary Oliver. Reprinted by permission of Houghton Mifflin Harcourt Publishing Company. All rights reserved.

"Luke" and "Percy, Waiting for Ricky" from *Red Bird* by Mary Oliver. Copyright © 2008 by Mary Oliver. Reprinted by permission of Beacon Press.

"Her Grave" from *New and Selected Poems, Volume One* by Mary Oliver. Copyright © 1992 by Mary Oliver. Reprinted by permission of Beacon Press.

"The Dog Has Run Off Again" from *West Wind: Poems and Prose Poems* by Mary Oliver. Copyright © 1997 by Mary Oliver. Reprinted by permission of Houghton Mifflin Company. All rights reserved.

"Holding on to Benjamin," "Percy," and "Little Dog's Rhapsody in the Night" from *New and Selected Poems, Volume Two* by Mary Oliver. Copyright © 2005 by Mary Oliver. Reprinted by permission of Beacon Press.

"School" (originally published as "Percy (Six)") from *Thirst* by Mary Oliver. Copyright © 2006 by Mary Oliver. Reprinted by permission of Beacon Press.

ALSO AVAILABLE

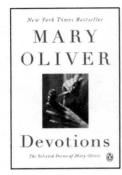

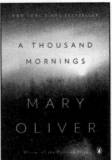

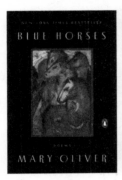

PENGUIN BOOKS